Cambridge Little Steps 3

Numeracy Book

Lorena Peimbert

CAMBRIDGE UNIVERSITY PRESS

Cambridge Little Steps 3

① Numbers 1 to 20

👁 Look. 2₃¹ Count. ✎ Write.

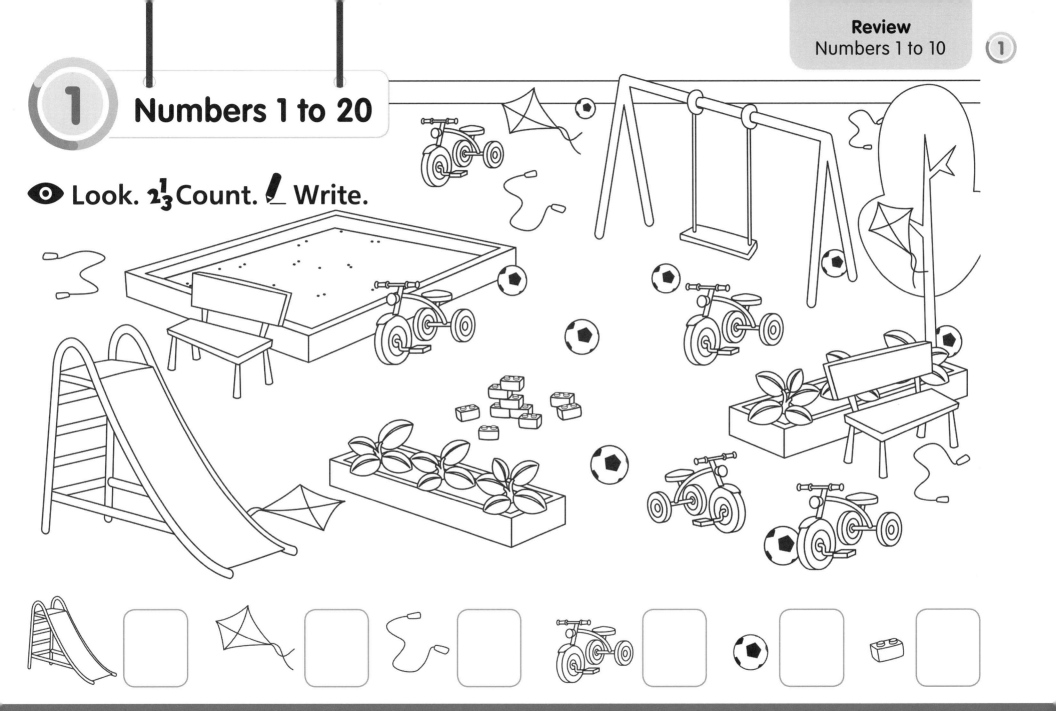

Presentation: Make a set of cards with one to ten objects found on a playground on each card (slide, kite, jump rope, tricycle, ball, blocks). Show children a card. Ask: *What's this? (A slide.) How many slides can you see?* Children count and say. Finally, children open their books and find and count each object in the picture. Then they write the correct number.
Practice: Give children a white sheet of paper and different-colored crayons. Put the cards you made inside a bag. Play some music. Have children pass around the bag. Stop the music. Have the child with the bag pull out a card, hold it up, and count the pictures on it. Children write the correct number on their sheet of paper using the color you say.

Trace. ➡➡ Follow. 2¹3 Count.

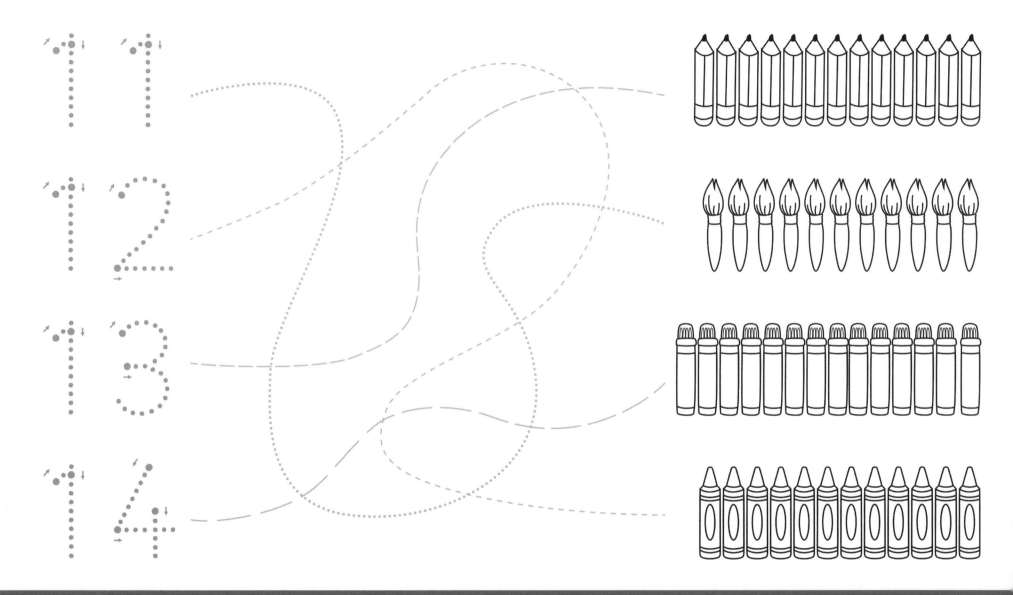

Presentation: Make a set of cards with eleven to fifteen school objects on each card (pencils, glue sticks, paintbrushes, scissors, and crayons). Show children a card. Ask: *What's this?* *(A pencil.) How many pencils can you see?* Children count and say. Finally, children open their books. They trace each number, follow the path, and count the school objects.
Practice: Display the cards facedown on the board at a height children can reach. Children go to the board and turn over a card. Then they count the pictures and write the correct number on the board.

 Look. 2$\frac{1}{3}$ Count. ✏ Color.

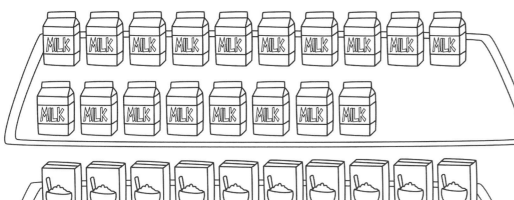

16 17 18 19 20

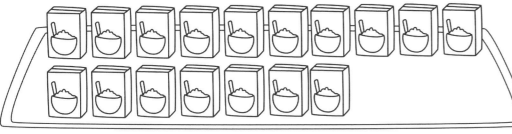

16 17 18 19 20

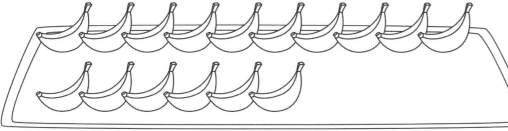

16 17 18 19 20

16 17 18 19 20

Presentation: Make a set of cards with sixteen to twenty food items on each card (cartons of milk, cereal boxes, apples, bananas, and pancakes). Show children a card. Ask: *What's this?* *(Milk.) How many cartons of milk can you see?* Children count and say. Finally, children open their books and count each group of food items. Then they color the corresponding number.
Practice: Display the cards on the board. Toss a ball to a child. The child says: *One.* That child tosses the ball to another child, who says: *Two.* Continue until a child says: *Sixteen.* That child goes to the board and circles a card with sixteen objects. Repeat to review numbers 17, 18, 19, and 20.

2⅓ Count. ✎ Write. ✏️ Draw.

2		4		6		8		10

11		13		15		17		19	

2 Numbers 21 to 30

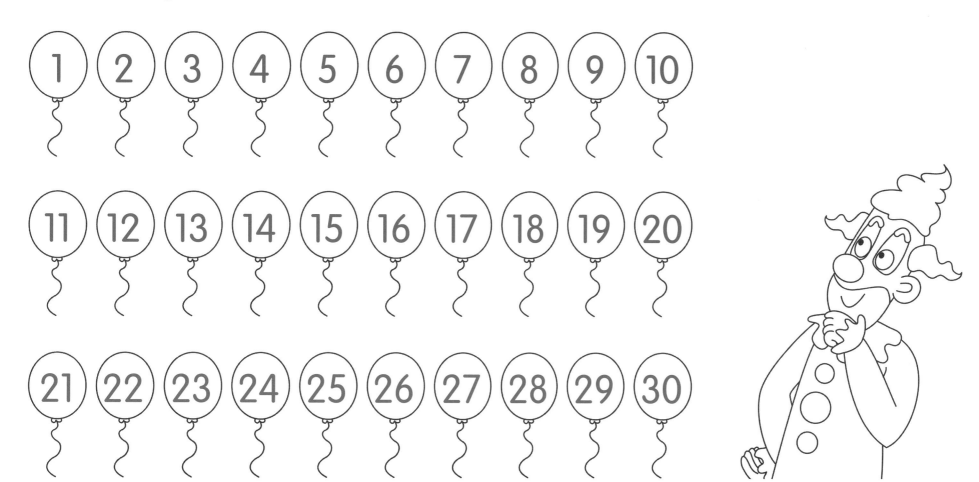

👁 Look. 2⅓ Count. ✏ Color.

Presentation: Make a set of cards with twenty-one to thirty balloons on each card and another set with a number between 21 and 30 on each card. Then show a card with balloons. Ask: *How many balloons are there? Let's count!* Finally, children open their books and count the balloons. Then they color the balloons with the numbers 21 to 30.
Practice: Place the number cards and the cards with the balloons facedown on the board. Divide the class into two teams. A child from one team turns over two cards. If they are a pair (a number card and a card with the corresponding number of balloons), the child takes the cards and earns a point for the team. The team with the most points wins the game.

7

2¹₃ Count. ◯ Trace. ✎ Write.

23

Presentation: Make a set of cards with twenty-one to twenty-five cupcakes on each card and a set of cards with a number between 21 and 25 on each card. Display the cards with cupcakes on the board in sequential order. Fan out the number cards in your hands. Invite a volunteer to choose a card. The child says the number and attaches it under the corresponding card on the board. Finally, children open their books. They count the cupcakes and trace or write the numbers.
Practice: Display the cupcake cards facedown on the board. Invite volunteers to turn over a card. The child counts the cupcakes and writes the corresponding number below.

²₃¹ Count. 📖 Match. ⬭ Trace.

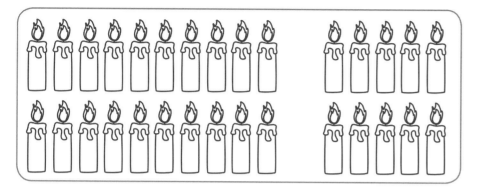

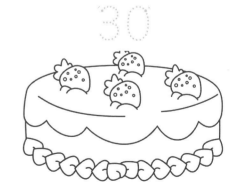

Presentation: Make a set of cards with twenty-six to thirty candles on each card. Show children a card. Ask: *How many candles can you see?* Children count and say. Invite a volunteer to write the number on the board. Finally, children open their books. They count and color the candles. Then they draw a line from each set of candles to the corresponding cake and trace the number.
Practice: Display all the cards on the board. Toss a ball to a child. The child says: *One.* That child tosses the ball to another child, who says: *Two.* Continue until a child says: *Twenty-six.* That child goes to the board and circles a card with twenty-six candles. Repeat to review numbers 27, 28, 29, and 30.

9

👁 Look. 2¹₃ Count. ⭘ Trace.

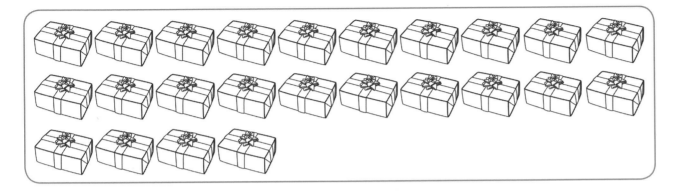

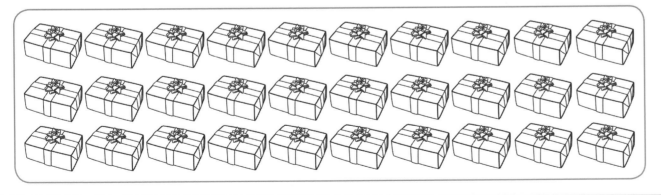

Presentation: Make a set of cards with twenty-one to thirty gifts on each card. Show children a card. Ask: *What's this? (A gift.) How many gifts can you see?* Children count and say. Finally, children open their books. They count the gifts in each row and then choose the correct number to trace.

Practice: Give children a white sheet of paper. Show children a card. Have them count the gifts to themselves and write the correct number on the paper. Then check that children wrote the correct numbers in the order you showed the cards.

3 Numbers 31 to 40

👁 Look. 2¹₃ Count. ⚪ Trace.

10

20

30

31 32 33 34 35

36 37 38 39 40

Presentation: Make a set of cards with a number between 31 and 40 on each card, and a set of cards with thirty-one to forty happy faces on each card, arranged in three rows of ten with the additional faces set apart. Display the number cards on the board. Hold up a card with happy faces. Count the happy faces with children. Then invite a volunteer to attach the card below the corresponding number on the board. Guide children to understand how to count by tens. Finally, children open their books, count, and trace the numbers.
Practice: Display the cards with happy faces facedown. Children go to the board and turn over a card. Then they count the faces and write the corresponding number on the board.

11

Draw. Trace. Count.

10

20

30

31   32   33   34   35

Presentation: Make a set of cards with a number between 31 and 35 on each card. Lead children in counting to thirty-five. Then hold up a card and have children say the number. Finally, children open their books. They draw a family member in each of the empty frames and trace the numbers. Then they count the family members on the page.

Practice: Draw groups of thirty-one to thirty-five shapes on the board. Invite a child to choose from the set of number cards. The child says the number, counts the shapes on the board, and attaches the card under the corresponding group of shapes.

2⅓ Count. ✏️ Draw. ⭕ Trace.

1	2	3	4	5	6	7	8	9	10
11	12	13	14	15	16	17	18	19	20
21	22	23	24	25	26	27	28	29	30
31	32	33	34	35	36	37	38	39	40

➡➡ Follow. ✏ Write. ⭕ Trace.

40

Presentation: Make various sets of cards of the numbers 1 to 40. Children sit in small groups, forming teams. Give each team a set of cards. Instruct children to put the cards in order. The first team to finish wins. Finally, children open their books. They count as they follow the path and write or trace the numbers to complete the sequence and reach the finish line.
Practice: Children sit in a circle. Give a child a ball. That child says: *One* and passes the ball to the child next to him or her. That child says: *Two,* and so on. Children continue passing the ball until a child says: *Forty.* If they miss a number, they have to start from the beginning.

4 Numbers 41 to 50

$2\frac{1}{3}$ Count. ✏ Color.

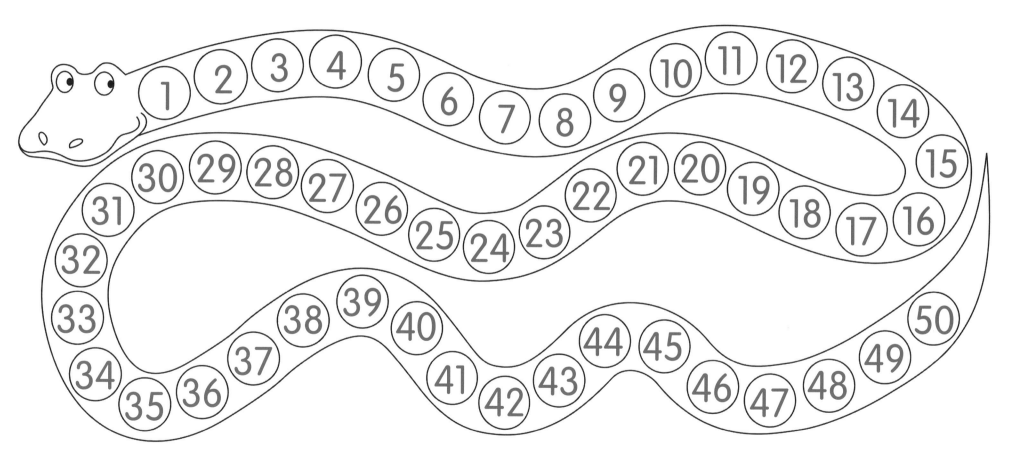

Presentation: Make a set of cards with forty-one to fifty circles on each card, distributing the circles in rows of ten with the additional circles set apart. Hold up each card and lead children in counting the circles. Guide children to understand how to count by tens and then count the additional circles. Finally, children open their books. They count and color numbers 41 to 50.
Practice: Put the cards with circles inside a bag. Play some music. Have children pass around the bag. Stop the music. The child with the bag pulls out a card, shows it to the class, and counts the circles.

2^1_3 Count. ✏ Write. ⬛ Match.

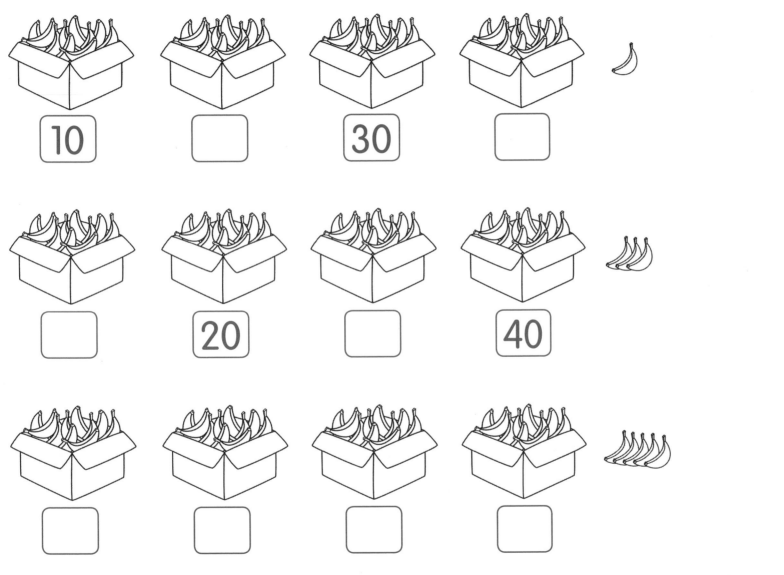

Presentation: Make a set of cards with forty-one to forty-five bananas on each card, distributing the bananas in rows of ten with the additional bananas set apart. Show children a card. Ask: *What are these? (Bananas.) How many bananas can you see?* Children count and say. Finally, children open their books. They write the missing numbers. Then they count the bananas, match the bananas to the corresponding number, and trace the number.
Practice: Display the cards facedown on the board at a height children can reach. Invite a volunteer to turn over a card. The child counts the pictures and writes the correct number below.

2⅓ Count. ✎ Write. ⬭ Trace.

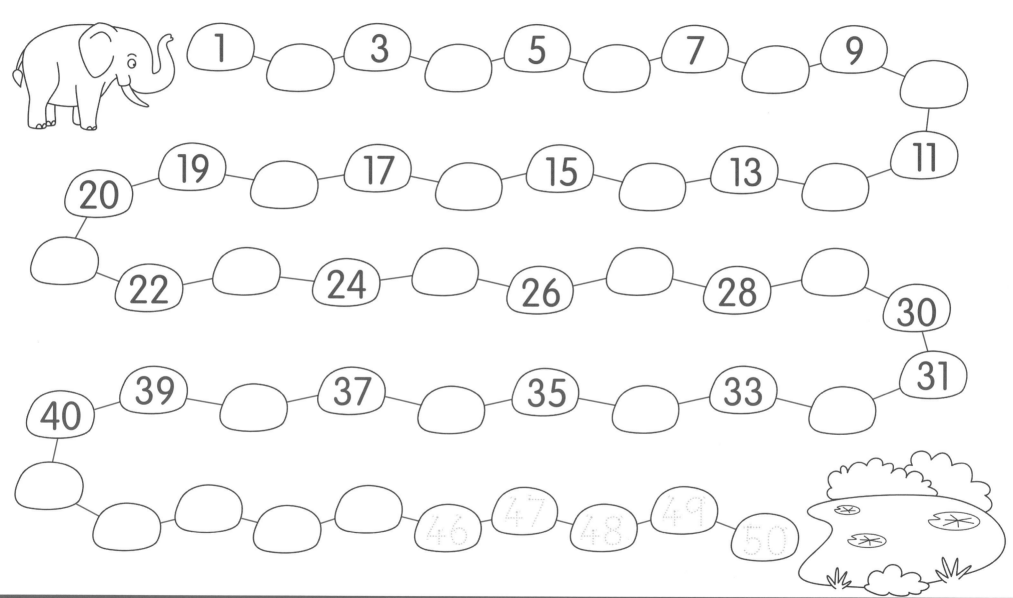

Presentation: Make a set of cards with a number from 1 to 50 on each card. Show children a card. Ask: *What number is this?* Children say the number. Finally, children open their books. They count and write or trace the missing numbers to help the elephant reach the lake and take a bath.
Practice: Display the number cards on the board. Point and count with children. Then toss a ball to a child. The child says: *One.* That child tosses the ball to another child, who says: *Two.* Children continue until they reach fifty. If a child misses a number, he or she goes to the board and circles that number. The game resumes starting from that number.

17

2⅓ Count. 🖊 Draw. ✏ Color.

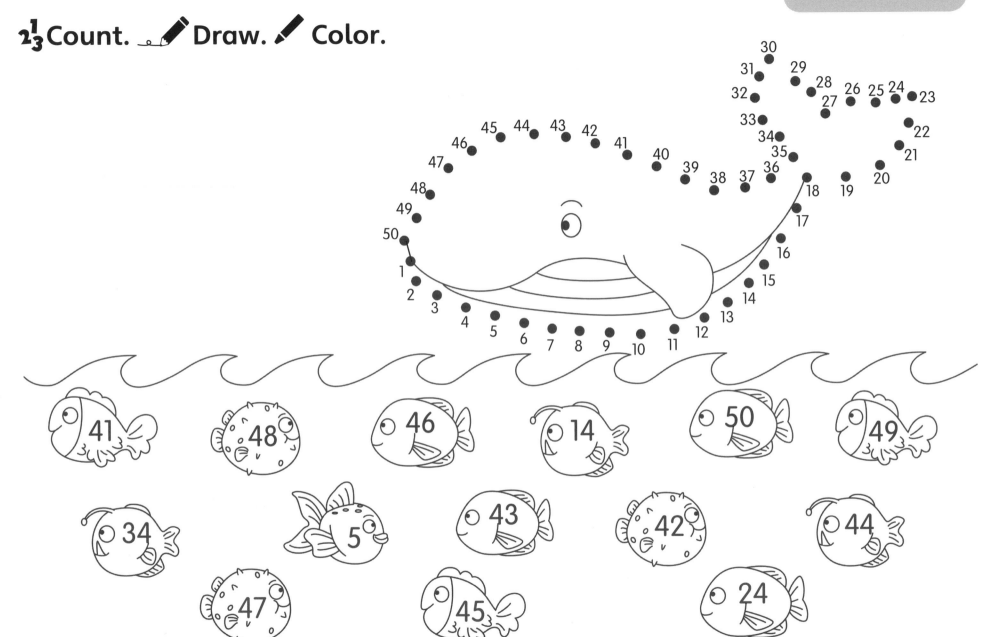

Presentation: Write numbers 1 to 40 on the board and lead children in saying each number. Ask: *What number comes next? (Forty-one.)* Call on a child to write the number on the board in the correct position. Continue until your reach 50. Finally, children open their books and count as they draw lines to connect the dots from 1 to 50. Then they color the fish with numbers 41 to 50.
Practice: Make various sets of cards with a number from 1 to 50 on each card. Divide the class into small groups and give each group a set of cards. At the count of three, children put the number cards in the correct order. The first team to finish wins the game. Finally, children count as they point to the corresponding cards.

5 Numbers 51 to 60

2¹/₃ Count. ✏ **Color.**

Presentation: Make a set of cards with fifty-one to sixty squares on each card, distributing the squares in rows of ten with the additional squares set apart. Hold up each card and lead children in counting the squares. Remind children how to count by tens and then count the additional squares. Finally, children open their books. They count and color numbers 51 to 60.
Practice: Give children a white sheet of paper and different-colored crayons. Put the cards with squares you made inside a bag. Play some music. Have children pass around the bag. Stop the music. Have the child with the bag pull out a card, hold it up, and count the squares on it. Children write the correct number on their sheet of paper using the color you say.

19

👁 Look. 2¹₃ Count. ◯ Trace.

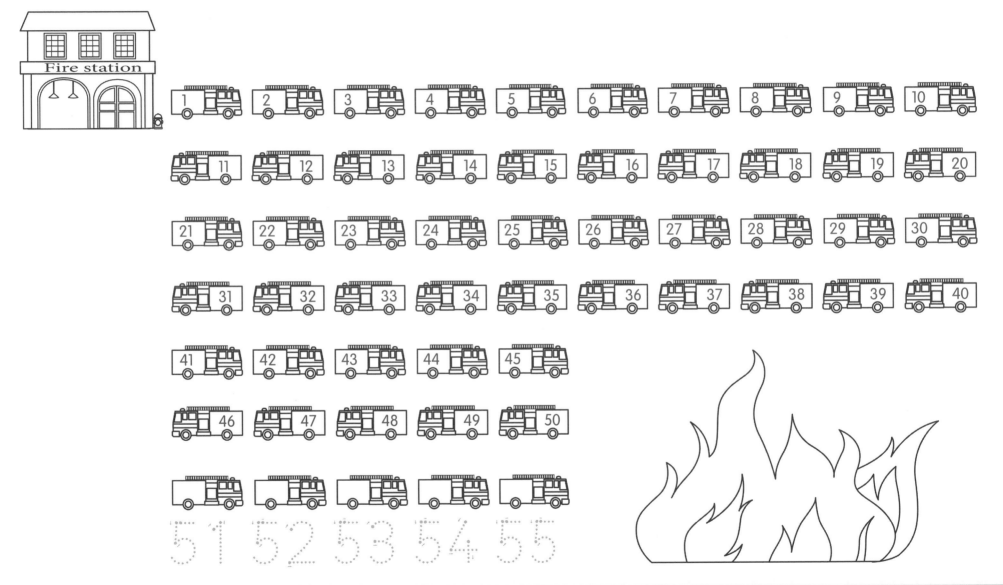

Presentation: Make a set of cards with fifty-one to fifty-five fire trucks on each card, distributing the trucks in rows of ten with the additional trucks set apart. Show children a card. Ask: *What are these? (Fire trucks.) How many fire trucks can you see?* Children count and say. Finally, children open their books, count the fire trucks, and trace numbers 51 to 55.

Practice: Display the cards facedown on the board at a height children can reach. Invite a volunteer to turn over a card. The child counts the pictures and writes the correct number below.

✎ Write. ◯ Trace. ▌Match.

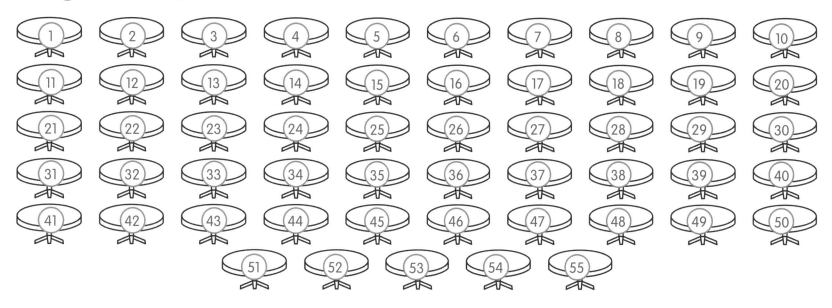

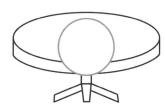 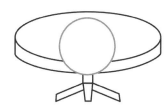 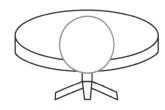 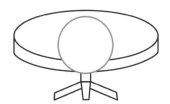 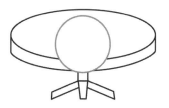

 60    58    56    57    59

Presentation: Make a set of cards with fifty-five to sixty tables on each card, distributing the tables in rows of ten with the additional tables set apart. Show children a card. Ask: *How many tables can you see?* Children count and say. Finally, children open their books and count the tables. Then they trace numbers 56 to 60 and match the waiters to the correct tables.
Practice: Put the cards with tables inside a bag. Play some music. Have children pass around the bag. Stop the music. The child with the bag pulls out a card, shows it to the class, and counts the tables. Then the child writes the number on the board.

21

👁 Look. 2¹₃ Count. ✏ Write.

Presentation: Make various sets of cards of numbers 1 to 60. Divide class into small groups. Give each team a set of fifty random cards plus ten blank cards. They put the cards in order and write the missing numbers to complete the sequence. Finally, children open their books. They count the people and objects called out at the bottom of the page and write the correct number.
Practice: Make a set of cards with fifty-one to sixty items on each card and a set with a number from 51 to 60. Display the cards around the classroom. Play some music as children pass around a ball. Stop the music and say a number from 51 to 60. The child with the ball looks for that card and a card with that number of items and displays the pair on the board.

6 Numbers 61 to 70

$2\frac{1}{3}$ Count. ✏ Color.

61 62 63 64 65 66 67 68 69 70

Presentation: Make a set of cards with sixty-one to seventy ice cubes on each card, distributing the cubes in rows of ten with the additional cubes set apart. Hold up each card and lead children in counting the ice cubes. Remind children how to count by tens and then count the additional ice cubes. Finally, children open their books. They count and color numbers 61 to 70.
Practice: Give children a white sheet of paper and different-colored crayons. Put the cards with ice cubes inside a bag. Play some music. Have children pass around the bag. Stop the music. Have the child with the bag pull out a card, hold it up, and count the pictures on it. Children write the correct number on their sheet of paper using the color you say.

2¹₃ Count. ✎ Write. ⟲ Trace.

Presentation: Make a set of cards with sixty-one to sixty-five scoops of ice cream. Show children a card. Ask: *What's this? (Ice cream.) How many scoops of ice cream can you see?* Children count and say. Finally, children open their books. Then they count and write or trace the missing numbers.

Practice: Display the cards with sixty-one to sixty-five scoops of ice cream facedown on the board at a height children can reach. Invite a volunteer to turn over a card, count the pictures, and write the correct number below.

2¹₃ Count. ✏ Write. ⬭ Trace.

10   [ ]   [ ]   [ ]   50   [ ]

[ ]   [ ]   [ ]   [ ]   [ ]   66   67   68   69   70

25

2$\frac{1}{3}$ Count. ◯ Circle.

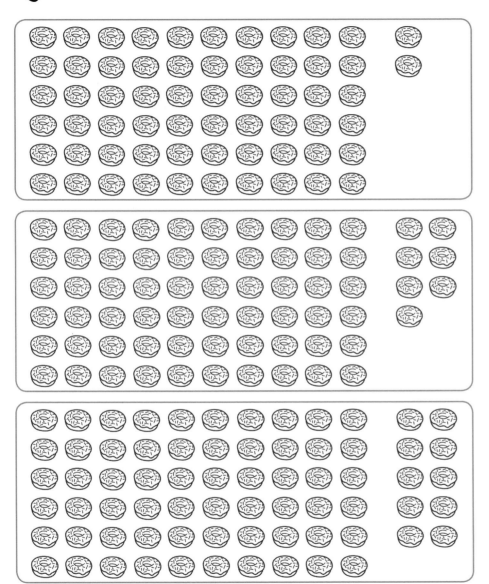

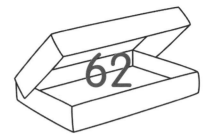

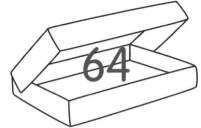

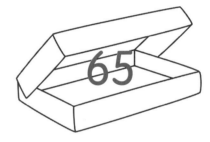

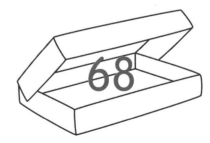

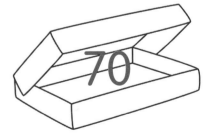

Presentation: Make a set of cards with sixty-one to seventy donuts on each card, distributing the donuts in rows of ten with the additional donuts set apart. Show children a card. Ask: *What are these? (Donuts.) How many donuts can you see?* Children count and say. Finally, children open their books. They count each set of donuts and circle the corresponding number.
Practice: Display the cards on the board. Divide the class into two teams. A child from each team goes to the back of the classroom. Say: *Touch sixty-one donuts!* Children walk quickly to the board and touch the corresponding card. If they do it correctly, they earn a point for their team. The team with the most points wins the game.

7 Numbers 71 to 80

2¹₃ Count.  Say.

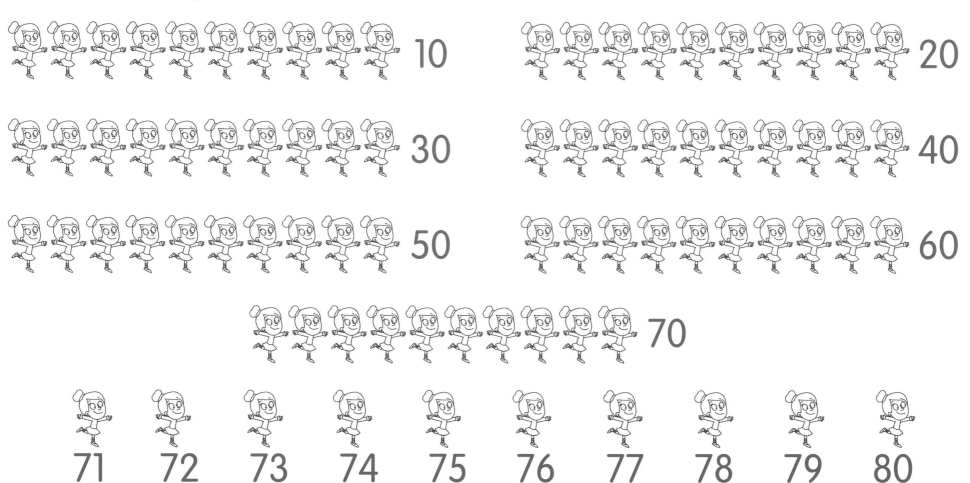

10

20

30

40

50

60

70

71 72 73 74 75 76 77 78 79 80

Presentation: Make a set of cards with seventy-one to eighty dancers on each card, arranged in rows of ten with the additional dancers set apart. Hold up each card and lead children in counting the dancers. Finally, children open their books and count the dancers. Then they say each number from 71 to 80.
Practice: Give children a white sheet of paper and different-colored crayons. Put the cards with dancers you made inside a bag. Play some music. Have children pass around the bag. Stop the music. Have the child with the bag pull out a card, hold it up, and count the dancers on it. Children write the correct number on their sheet of paper using the color you say.

2¹₃ Count. ✎ Color. ⬭ Trace.

71 72 73 74 75

Presentation: Make a set of cards with a number between 71 and 75 on each card and write numbers 71 to 75 on the board. Lead children in counting to seventy-five. Then hold up a card. Have children say the number and write it under your number on the board. Finally, children open their books. They count and color the balls up to 70. Then they count and color the balls from 71 to 75 and trace the numbers.

Practice: Give children some clay or play dough. Say a number from 71 to 75 and have them form the number.

2¹₃ Count. ◯ Trace. ✏ Draw.

10

20

30

40

50

60

70

71 72 73 74 75

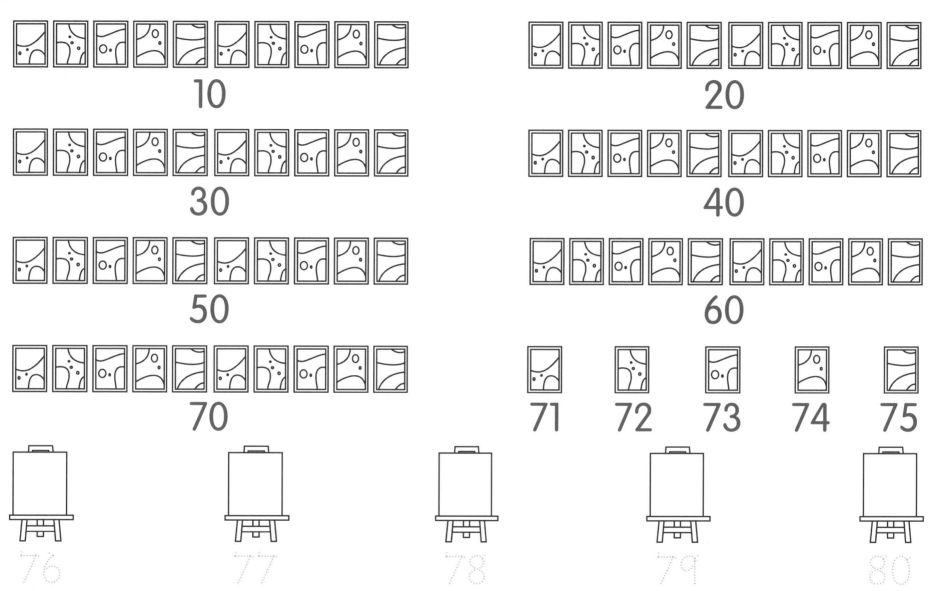

76   77   78   79   80

Presentation: Lead children in counting to eighty. Write the numbers 10, 20, 30, 40, 50, 60, 70, and 76 to 80 on the board. Point to each number and ask a volunteer to say the number and trace it in the air. Finally, children open their books. They count to seventy-five and trace numbers 76 to 80 as they say each number aloud. Then children draw a picture on each easel.
Practice: Give children a sheet of paper each. Have them choose a number from 76 to 80, write the number, and decorate it as if it were a piece of art. Ask volunteers to show their pieces of art and say the number they drew. Display their numbers around the classroom.

29

2⅓ Count. ✏️ Draw. 🗨️ Say.

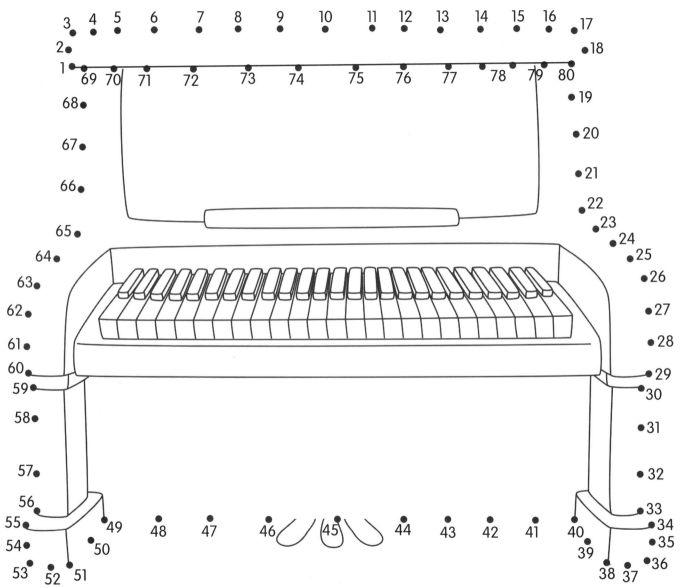

Presentation: Write numbers 1 to 70 on the board and lead children in saying each number. Ask: *What number comes next? (Seventy-one.)* Call on a child to say the number and then write it on the board in the correct position. Continue until your reach eighty. Finally, children open their books and connect the dots to complete the picture as they say each number aloud.
Practice: Toss a ball to a child. The child says: *One.* That child tosses the ball to another child, who says: *Two.* Continue until a child says: *Seventy-one.* That child writes the number on the board. Continue to review numbers 72 through 80.

8 Numbers 81 to 90

👁 Look. 2¹₃ Count. ✏ Color.

10

20

30

40

50

60

70

80

81 82 83 84 85 86 87 88 89 90

Presentation: Make a set of cards with numbers 10, 20, 30, 40, 50, 60, 70, and 80, and a set with a number between 81 and 90, on each card. Display the cards. Lead children in counting by tens up to eighty and then from eighty-one to ninety as you point to each card. Finally, children open their books and count the frogs. Then they count from 81 to 90 and color in the numbers and the frogs.
Practice: Give children a white sheet of paper and different-colored crayons. Put the cards you made with numbers 81 to 90 inside a bag. Play some music. Have children pass around the bag. Stop the music. Have the child with the bag pull out a card, hold it up, and say the number. Children write the correct number on their sheet of paper using the color you say.

31

2¹₃ Count. ✏ Write. ✏ Color.

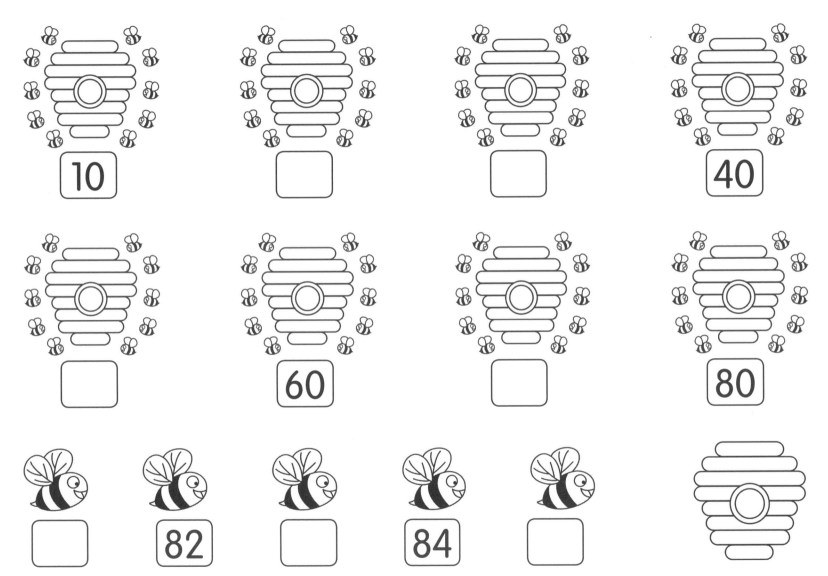

10			40
	60		80

| | 82 | | 84 | |

Presentation: Make a set of cards with a number between 81 and 85 on each card and write numbers 81 to 85 on the board. Lead children in counting to eighty-five. Then hold up a card. Have children say the number and write it under your number on the board. Finally, children open their books. They count the bees and write the missing numbers. Then they color the bees at the bottom of the page.
Practice: Display the cards from 81 to 85 facedown on the board at a height children can reach. Invite a volunteer to turn over a card and say the correct number.

2¹⁄₃ Count. ✎ Write. ⬭ Trace.

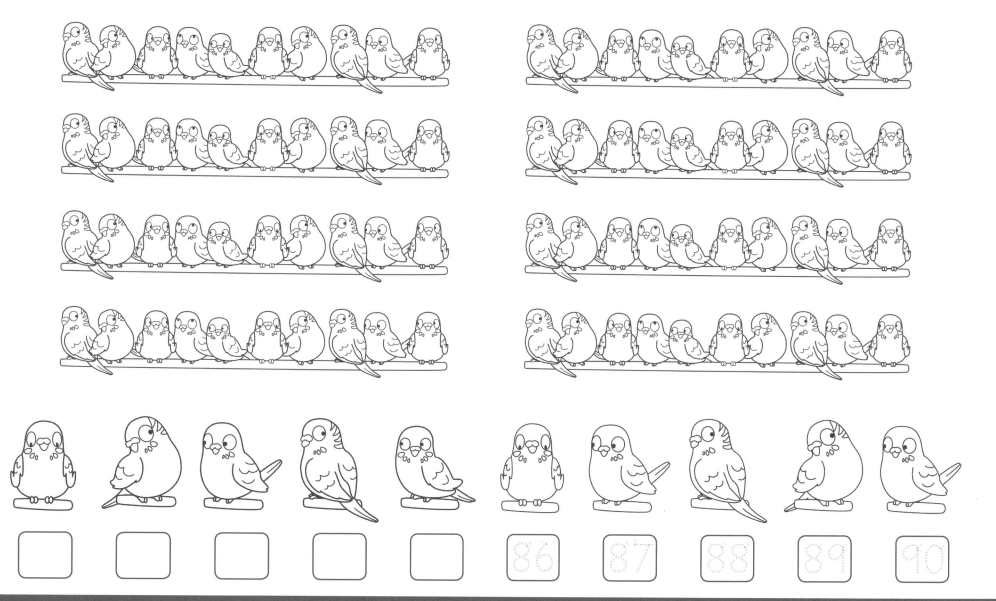

86 87 88 89 90

Presentation: Make a set of cards with a number from 86 to 90 on each card. Show children a card. Ask: *What number is this?* Children say the number. Finally, children open their books. They count the birds and write or trace the missing numbers. Then children color the birds for numbers 81–90.
Practice: Display the cards with numbers 86 to 90 on the board. Divide the class into two teams. A child from each team goes to the back of the classroom. Call out a number from 86 to 90. Children walk quickly to touch the corresponding card. Each child who touches the correct card earns a point for his or her team. The team with the most points wins the game.

33

👁 Look. 2¹₃ Count. 🃏 Match.

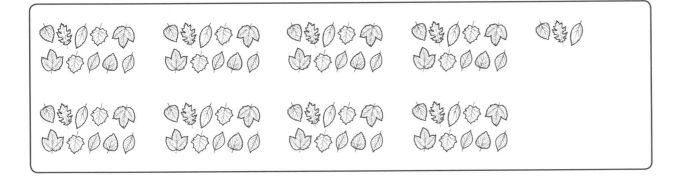

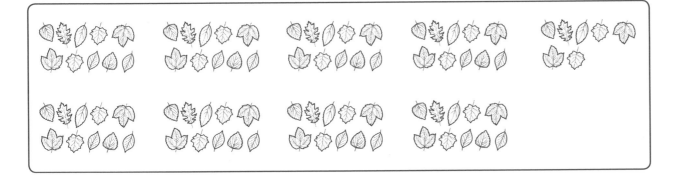

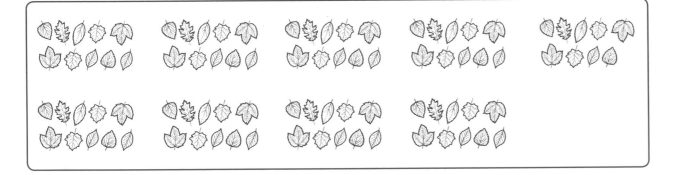

Presentation: Write the number *80* on the board and have children say the number aloud. Ask: *What number comes next? (Eighty-one.)* Call on a child to say the number and write it on the board after the number *80*. Continue until your reach ninety. Finally, children open their books. They count the leaves in each row and draw a line to match the leaves to the corresponding tree.
Practice: Make a set of cards with a number between 81 and 90 on each, and a set of cards with eight-one to ninety leaves on each, distributing the leaves in rows of ten with the additional leaves set apart. Place the cards facedown on the board. Invite a child to turn over two cards. If the number and the number of leaves on the cards match, the child takes the pair.

Numbers 91 to 100

2¹₃ Count. ✏ Write. 🖍 Color.

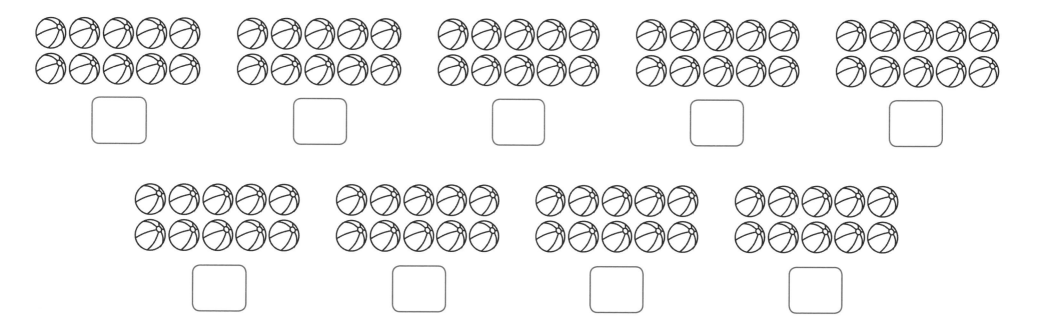

| 91 | 92 | 93 | 94 | 95 | 96 | 97 | 98 | 99 | 100 |

Presentation: Make a set of cards with numbers 10, 20, 30, 40, 50, 60, 70, 80, and 90, and a set with a number from 91 to 100. Lead children in counting by tens up to ninety and from ninety-one to one hundred as you point to each card. Finally, children open their books and count the beach balls. They write the missing numbers and color numbers 91 to 100.
Practice: Give children a white sheet of paper and different-colored crayons. Put the cards you made with numbers 91 to 100 inside a bag. Play some music. Have children pass around the bag. Stop the music. Have the child with the bag pull out a card, hold it up, and say the number. Children write the correct number using the color you say.

2¹₃ Count. ✎ Write. ⬭ Trace.

	10
	50

91   92   93   94   95

Presentation: Make a set of cards with a number from 91 to 95 on each card. Diplay the cards in random order. Say a number from 91 to 95. A volunteer traces the number with his or her finger. Finally, children open their books. They count the flashlights in each row and write the correct number in the box. Then they continue counting, trace the numbers, and color the pictures.
Practice: Children sit in a circle. Give a child a ball. That child says: *One* and passes the ball to the child next to him or her. That child says: *Two*, and so on. Children continue passing the ball until a child says: *Ninety-five*. If they miss a number, they start over.

$2\frac{1}{3}$ Count. ✎ Write. ◯ Trace.

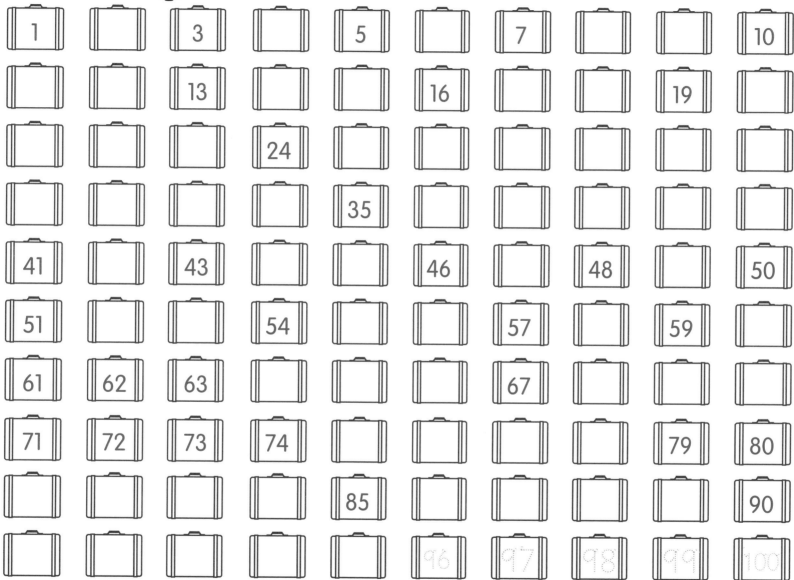

1		3		5		7			10
		13			16			19	
			24						
				35					
41		43			46		48		50
51			54			57		59	
61	62	63				67			
71	72	73	74					79	80
				85					90
					96	97	98	99	100

Presentation: Make a set of cards with ninety-one to one hundred suitcases on each card, distributing the suitcases in rows of ten with the additional suitcases set apart. Show children a card.
Ask: *What are these? (Suitcases.) How many suitcases can you see?* Children count and say. Finally, children open their books. They count the suitcases and write or trace the missing numbers.
Practice: Make various sets of cards with a number from 1 to 100 on each card. Have children sit in small groups, forming teams. Give each team a set of cards. When you say *Go!*, children have to put the cards in order. The team that finishes first wins.

37

👁 Look. 2¹₃ Count. ➡➡ Follow.

Presentation: Make a set of cards with a number between 91 and 100 on each card. Lead children in counting to one hundred. Then hold up a card and have children say the number. Finally, children open their books. They count and follow the maze to help the children reach the campsite.

Practice: Give children some clay or play dough. Say a number from 91 to 100 and have them form the number.